It's not all
Airy-Fairy Loads of Crap

It's not all
Airy-Fairy Loads of Crap

A Not-too-Serious Perspective
on Modern Spirituality

Julie Rasmussen

Red Renegade Press

It's not all Airy-Fairy Loads of Crap-A Not-too-Serious Perspective on Modern Spirituality

Published by Red Renegade Press 2021
Copyright ©2021 Julie Rasmussen. All rights reserved.

No part of this book may be reproduced in any form or by any mechanical means, including information storage and retrieval systems without permission in writing from the publisher/author, except by a reviewer who may quote passages in a review.

All images, logos, quotes, and trademarks included in this book are subject to use according to trademark and copyright laws of the United States of America.

> Publisher's Cataloging-in-Publication data
> Rasmussen, Julie.
> It's not all Airy-Fairy Loads of Crap-A Not-too-Serious Perspective on Modern Spirituality / Julie Rasmussen.
> p. cm.
> ISBN 978-0-578-34709-7

All rights reserved by Julie Rasmussen and Red Renegade Press.

This book is printed in the United States of America.

Correspondence may be sent to: redrenegadepress@gmail.com

Red Renegade Press

For Ned

"Believe nothing, no matter where you read it, or who said it ... unless it agrees with your own reason and your own common sense."
—Buddha

contents

introduction · 11

one: defining the undefinable · 14

two: the soup of love · 17

three: not dead, just dormant · 23

four: a meditation on meditation · 29

five: enlightenment and potato salad · 35

six: i forsee a slurpee ... · 41

seven: petey, the chicken killer · 45

eight: those things we do · 50

nine: james bond and salsa recipes	54
ten: #cleavageandcobbsalads	58
eleven: meat me in yoga class ... or not	62
twelve: assholes, creeps, and dipshits	67
thirteen: ned	72
fourteen: the vibrational crockpot	76
fifteen: you had me at namaste	80
sixteen: the times they are a changin'	87

introduction

I use irreverent titles for my books to keep things light.

Spirituality doesn't have to be such a serious subject.

Being spiritual doesn't require becoming a self-absorbed bore.

My first book, *I Didn't Believe any of this Hippie Dippy Bulls**t Either—A Skeptic's Awakening to the Spiritual Universe,* was a memoir of my own spiritual awakening, when I discovered that I am not a human having a spiritual experience, but rather that I am a *spiritual* being having a *human* experience. And the response I got from readers was that many of you had similar experiences, in one form or another.

I was so pleased to hear from all you brilliant folks out there who had also once thought that talk of "alignment" and "vibes" was solely for nuts and flakes ... yet, who were now spiritually curious or woke, as well.

My own experience, and your positive response, have deepened my desire to broaden my spirituality understanding. So let's use this fun size book to explore some of the lingo, myths, and mystery surrounding certain subjects, and take a realistic look at what living a modern spiritual life really means.

Now, as we dive into these ramblings, please note this:

I never claim to be some fully-enlightened Guru, *nor* am I claiming to be the President of Spirituality, representing *all* spiritualists. No, these are just humorous commentaries, written from my own perspective and experience.

God knows, they're not gospel on anything.

I'm just a communicator who likes to hear myself talk, writing the practical books that I wish were around when I started down my spiritual path.

Consider me your equally curious tour guide, map in hand, observing and trying to decipher the truth with a healthy balance of emotion and common sense as we go along.

And as always, I lovingly encourage you to do the same as you read. Use this book as a catalyst to decide *your* own truths, because neither I, nor anyone else, can tell you what hard-core fact is on most of these topics.

In *Hippie Dippy Bulls**t,* we cracked the door open with the ego, soulmates, numerology, synchronicities, and the Law of Attraction, but there's still much more to explore about this enormous spectrum of modern spirituality.

So loosen up, prepare to expand your mind, and let's go see

what we can discover ... together.

And I absolutely promise not to get too serious.

chapter one

***

defining the undefinable

There is no one singular theology in "spirituality," which makes it hard to even define. So maybe clarifying what spirituality is *not* is a good place to start.

It's not a religion. It has no governing body, no written codes of conduct, no formal leadership, nor any one doctrine to follow. It's not the organized worship of any specific God or religious figure, but rather it's a personal spiritual *practice.*

There's a whole spectrum of people and practices that can fall under the label of spirituality.

Somewhere on that spectrum are those who practice meditation, understand the Law of Attraction (that our thoughts attract all of our life experiences), and who study the master teachers, from the historical to the popular modern.

Others on the spectrum connect more directly with the non-physical world, like psychics, mediums, and channelers.

Then there are mind and body energy healers, whose focus is more on things like reiki, hypnotherapy, and/or yoga.

Those who have an interest in the more scientific realm of spirituality, the study of consciousness as energy and quantum physics, are on the spectrum as well.

And finally, there are those whose practice is more among the planets and the stars, in our spiritual connection to other planets and the entire universe.

Try explaining all of that in a tri-fold, glossy pamphlet.

As I found myself exploring the spectrum of spirituality through books and workshops, I can't say that I found truth in everything that I read or heard, but I also didn't feel any pressure to do so. This journey is all about discovering your own truths. And yes, some spiritualists' practices do include things like astrology, crystals, and/or dressing like Stevie Nicks from the '70s, but those things are not required, unless they have meaning to you.

Your definition of spirituality is what resonates with *you*.

I think most all spiritual and religious teachings are saying the same three things; they're just being said with variation, depending on the teacher, the time period, and the culture.

1. That we are all consciousness, we are more than our human bodies. We are souls.

2. That a supreme, omniscient presence exists in the universe.

3. That we can connect to that supreme, omniscient pres-

ence by following certain practices.

Often, in religion, those practices are taught as ways of behaving—obeying commandments or rules, performing rituals, or praying. In spirituality that connection is usually sought through meditation.

Religion and spirituality aren't foes. My own path went through religion before I came to spirituality. They're just different paths that people take while seeking the answers to life's eternal questions: "Where did I come from?" "Why am I here?" and "What happens when I die?"

Religion just often includes the worship or acceptance of one deity and doctrine, formed around one teacher's experience, to answer those questions ... while spirituality is answering them through your own personal connection with Source, and often, guidance from a variety of teachings.

Or as Deepak Chopra says perfectly, and in far less words, "Religion is belief in someone else's experience. Spirituality is having your own experience."

chapter two

***

the soup of love

I magine a large, blank whiteboard in front of you.

At the very bottom of the board, take your blue and green markers and draw half a sphere (split horizontally) that looks like the earth.

Next, draw a large, low-hanging, gray cloud just above the earth, left to right, across the whole board. Fill that cloud with words like: "separation, worry, lack, comparison," any and all the lousy, fear-based messages you can think of.

Above that gray cloud, leave some white space, and at the top of the board, draw some golden yellow smiley faces (I'm serious).

Now draw a ladder, resting on the earth that goes up, up, up through the gray cloud ... and into those golden smiley faces.

The smiley faces represent the soup of consciousness that we all come from. In this book, I'm mostly going to call that "Source."

I'm going to steer away from using the term "God" as much as possible for the simple reason that it conjures up the image of an authoritative, judgmental male figure for many people, and what I am talking about is not that version of God. Even for myself, the word "God" takes me back to a too human-like version of God that I no longer find accurate.

Author Marianne Williamson, in her book, *A Return to Love*, describes how that version of God originated, "Because we are angry and judgmental, we have projected those characteristics onto Him. We have made God up in *our* image."

Simply stated, God made man perfect in his image ... and in return, our egos made God shitty like us.

Knowing what we know about the ego these days, it's not hard at all to understand why we ended up with that version of an egoic God throughout history. Man has been projecting his ego all over God since the beginning of time. It's just what the ego does ... hijacks every good thing and mucks it all up with fear.

But let's let go of the past, and that old version of God right here. Let's start thinking of God as "Source energy," a ginormous mass of love energy that is the origin, or source, of all things. No judgment, no condemnation, no separation from us involved. Just a soup of positive, unconditional love energy.

I like to think of us humans as balloon people.

An empty balloon is the form that gets filled, just like our human bodies.

Our balloons get filled with energy—it is not newly created energy—it is just energy taken from the ginormous mass of love and relocated. The same energy that is in the balloon is still outside the balloon as well. Our balloons are now extensions, or expressions, of Source energy in physical form.

We putz around in our balloon bodies, taking in life experiences in physical form. Our balloon bodies allow us to enjoy other forms filled with Source energy, as well. We putz around until eventually our balloon body starts to wear out, or gets unexpectedly eaten by the dog, and our energy gets released to fully rejoin the ginormous mass again.

The Law of Conservation of Mass implies mass can neither be created nor destroyed, although it may be rearranged in space, or the entities associated with it may be changed in form. So, if you think of Source as the energy that we all come from, you can see that none of us are ever truly created or destroyed, we just change forms or get re-arranged at times.

Ok, so let's go back to the whiteboard.

Now draw yourself standing on the earth, in your balloon body. That's you—Source energy, now filling a form.

Here's what awakening is:

Your balloon form is born under the gray cloud of fear ... *unaware* that there is a cloud of fear. Very quickly, your smiling, loving balloon-self begins to absorb the fear cloud messages that say things like, "You're separate from God. Don't trust strangers. Conform. Wait for the other shoe to drop. Life is suffering."

Now draw your balloon-self frowning, lying on the earth,

smothered by the fear cloud, feeling a sense of hopeless separation from joy.

Awakening tends to happen to people when that fear cloud has got them so separated from Source energy that life feels like either intolerable suffering or chronic discontentment. Suffering is often the catalyst for awakening—you get so disillusioned or dissatisfied in the fear cloud that either you physically die, emotionally shut down ... or you awaken.

If you awaken, as I did, it means you have a shift in conscious understanding. You awaken to realizing you've been living in the fear cloud. It's as if your soul finally bursts through your ego and you find yourself high on that ladder, above the fear cloud, able to see that it, and your own ego, exist.

That's when things start getting good.

The world looks different. You are now up the ladder, seeing all the insanity from a broader perspective. You start to see how mankind's collective fear cloud (especially abundant in news, social media, and advertising) fills us with negative, bullshit beliefs about ourselves and each other.

You see why you felt so lousy.

Also, now up the ladder, you finally feel reconnected with the Source from which you came ... and it is divine bliss!

It's Nirvana. It is the peace that transcends all understanding. *Now* the religious and spiritual teachers, past and present, finally start making sense. You get it. *This* is the connection that they were talking about! It's about going home to the eternal goodness of it all.

Congratulations! Great News! You've just had a glimpse of enlightenment. Here's the not-so-great news ... you're likely to go down the ladder before you get back up again.

Wonk ... wonk ... wonnnnk ... (downer music).

Occasionally, you do hear stories of people awakening high up the ladder, and mostly staying there. I think for most, though, the experience is this: two steps up, one step back ... three steps up, one plummet to the bottom ... slow and awkward, especially at the beginning.

Why does it happen this way? Because we have to unlearn the fear cloud beliefs that we picked up in life. You can't hang out on the top rungs of the ladder while still holding beliefs from the bottom rungs.

You could label the ladder rungs as the spectrum of emotions. The bottom one is fear, then up you go to hate, anger, resentment, acceptance, hope, love, and eventually to unconditional love at the very top. You could absolutely refer to these emotions as "vibrations" as well. Bad vibes to good vibes, it's the same thing—vibrations are just emotions.

So, stand back and look at your whiteboard. How do you know where you are on the ladder? By how you feel. When you're full of worry and feel like shit, you're at the bottom, hanging out in the fear cloud. When you feel good to great, you're above the fear cloud, close to Source.

My own awakening experience shot me to the top for a glimpse of Heaven on earth ... and then back to the bottom, to start the climb again (and again and again). What was happening, was that with every rung that I went up (because, *hell ya*, I wanted to get back to the top), my ego would try to hold me back with fear messages. Our egos don't want what's good for us—they're crybabies, they want what they already know, the bottom of the ladder.

Spiritualists call that "resistance" ... and it sucks.

So how do you get unstuck from annoying resistance holding you on a low rung?

Well, that's the million-dollar question that mankind has been trying to answer since we first developed self-awareness.

I do have some answers for you, most of which require patience ... which you're going to exercise right now, as I tell you we'll get to more on this subject later.

chapter three

***

not dead, just dormant

My son, Alex and I were waiting at a stoplight near a city park one day a few years ago. Bored, we both glanced over to see some golfers in a fairway, with a cemetery next to it, and a split rail fence between the two.

"You know, that fence isn't keeping golf balls out of the cemetery or ghosts off the golf course," he commented to me, adding, "With the right attitude, they could combine the two."

We have got to be two of the most casual people on the planet about death. Not because we're insensitive, we've lost loved ones like everyone else, but because we both believe that the death transition is just a natural, eternal fact to be accepted.

And yes, Alex is still as unique and impressive as ever. He's a chill, responsible young adult who doesn't get riled up about much, except when I purposely roll my 'r's when ordering in Mexican restaurants, if I accidentally tune into a country music station, or when he sees the font **comic sans** used in public places.

Those seem to be his only hot buttons.

He's been on some book tour road trips out west with me the past few years, perfectly serving as my navigator, snack-retriever, and intellectual stimuli. We've made lasting memories as we've crossed state lines—me driving, and him designing jewelry out of our used pistachio shells. We travel well together, mutually agreeing to stop at interesting attractions like Frank Lloyd Wright's Talieson West in Scottsdale, The Neon Museum in Las Vegas (it was made *crystal fucking clear*, however, that I was on my own for *Donnie & Marie Live* while there) … and of course, The Museum of Death in Los Angeles.

Sometimes we'll discuss our own funeral plans on road trips, as it's always good to let someone else know your wishes, and because there's no one else around to judge us for our twisted ideas.

The last time we discussed it, Alex told me that he wants his funeral in a church with pews and a high ceiling.

He wants all the lights to be off and for his guests to each be given a lit candle as they file in.

"As the crowd grows and candlelight fills the room … they will all begin to look up … and see my dead body, dressed like like Pennywise (the evil clown from *It)*, rocking in a rocking chair up front," he says.

His ideas are usually a bit macabre.

Personally, I would like a realistic, full-size wax figure of myself cheerfully greeting my guests at the door as they enter my funeral.

I shouldn't say Alex and I are *the* most casual people on earth about death, there's also Barb. Barb is a dear friend of mine and the best high school science teacher in Iowa. She teaches anatomy and can dissect any fetal creature or nasty thing while eating a sandwich and not bat an eye. Her funeral plans are for her dead body to be taken back to her family farm and thrown into manure to disintegrate the flesh.

She then later wants her bones hosed down, hung nicely, and brought back to the high school … to be used as the science room skeleton for future generations.

That's the spirit of what I'm talking about.

Let's put the fun back in funeral!

Let's stop being so offended and violated by death. I think we're suffering more than necessary because of our egoic views on death.

I believe death is a direct, first-class, free drinks and free wifi flight to the very top of the ladder. It is the ultimate release and relief for the one who dies (I base my belief on the thousands of testimonies of people who've had near-death-experiences and on other modern spiritual teachings).

There are no rules about the how or when death can happen, and some of the greatest suffering we cause ourselves is trying to say there are.

To ever say a death is "unfair" is only looking at it through the pain of your separation, which is understandable … because it felt unfair to *you*.

And rightfully so at times. Some deaths just seem cruel and pointless from our human point of view. But I think Source would never agree with that perspective, or that "when" or "how" a death happens matters, either. To Source, death is just the soul's transition out of its current physical form, fully back to non-physical energy.

It's a warm welcome home party for the soul and *that's* what matters.

And just because someone's lifetime didn't last as long as you thought it should doesn't make that death wrong or a mistake. It just means they had a shorter lifetime than you expected. Why did they? Well, that's between them and Source. It's not personal or about you, so don't even try to use your ego to understand it. Rather, respect the death, lovingly grieve, and be grateful that you had them as long you did. And when you're ready, try allowing in a new, non-physical relationship with them, because as Mitch Albom wrote in his book, *Tuesdays with Morrie*,

"Death ends a life, not a relationship."

I personally believe that at the top of the ladder there's a revolving door that never stops. Many Eastern practices believe in reincarnation, as do I. I think we keep coming back for another round of life. We have that welcome home party in the clubhouse, then jump back in for another 18 holes (or whatever we can get).

I think prior to awakening, I couldn't accept the idea of reincarnation because it was so devastatingly offensive to my ego that it could have ever been, or will be in the future, *non-existant or someone else*.

"BUT, BUT, BUT … *I'M ME!*" my ego would gasp at her

eternal insignificance.

I also had problems with reincarnation when I was living in the fear cloud because I thought that life, well, sucked in many ways. I wanted to believe death was finally relief from all the suffering of (groan) life.

I'd rather go somewhere unknown and hope for the best, than come back to this shit show, I thought at times.

It wasn't until I awakened, and saw life through the eyes of Source, that I saw we don't need to die to escape suffering. We can manage our human suffering by accepting that all things, good and bad, are just a part of the whole life experience.

It's only our *resistance* to anything that feels bad.

Suffering has deep purpose on the cosmic scale. It causes us to reach for a bigger understanding of the universe. It helps us to expand our compassion for others. Suffering gives us contrast—without it, we wouldn't even know what well-being is. And death is no different, it gives us necessary perspective and adds value to life. It's part of the divine design and perfection of our existence, just as much as birth is.

And upon going home and returning fully to Source energy, we remember that life is absolutely *not* a shit show. Back in the bliss, I think we eagerly choose to keep coming back to earth because there's serious creation and fun to be had.

I think we *want* to be here as expressions of Source in our balloon forms. And why wouldn't we? The diverse people, places, nature, music, art, comedy, technology, etc … they're all here for us to play with.

We come for the crisp sound of a drumline in a marching band, for the smell of campfires, and for the visual delight of fireworks against a black summer sky. We come for the pleasures of sex, warm beaches, fresh guacamole, and Tom Hanks movies.

We come for the *whole* life experience, and I think death is the last thing we're thinking about when we decide to do it again … and the last thing we should waste our days here overly focused on.

How utterly ridiculous it is to spend a life worrying about death, when you really think about it.

Alex would like his tombstone to read, "Not dead, just dormant."

I think I'll go with that one, too. Death is only the end of one's lifetime, but not of one's existence.

You can't kill a soul.

I'll be back, because this is where the good stuff is, and I want to get my hands in the clay over and over again.

Seeing the bigger picture of the natural divinity of death could help us all suffer less, enjoy life more, and realize something sublime …

That this *is* Heaven.

chapter four

***

a meditation on meditation

Grab a pillow, and let's meditate on meditation.

Meditation, in large part, was introduced to America through Paramahansa Yogananda, an Indian Hindu monk, guru, and yogi. He introduced millions to the teachings of meditation and yoga from 1920 to 1952 through public talks and gatherings. In 1946, his book, *Autobiography of a Yogi,* was published to critical acclaim and has since sold millions.

On meditation, Yogananda said, "It is the most practical science in the world. Most people would want to meditate if they understood it's value and experienced its beneficial effects. The ultimate object of meditation is to attain conscious awareness of God, and of the soul's eternal oneness with Him."

There are technically seven different types of meditation,

each having slightly different focuses and practices, but to keep things simple here, I'm just talking about meditation in general. The purpose of meditation is to get yourself into a mental state that connects you to the bigger picture of who you are—an extension of Source energy.

It's a brief, rejuvenating hiatus from our resistance and incessant thinking. It's a recharge for the mind, body, and soul.

I'd love to tell you that I'm a mediation expert, and here's how to do it in three easy steps ... except that my meditations very often go like this:

"Ok meditation, take me away." ... (breeeeeeeathe) ... "Damn, I forgot to buy kitty litter." ... (breeeeeathe) ... "And Nutella! Damn! Damn!" ... (breeeeethe) ... "Nutella tastes like chocolate frosting." ... (breeeethe) ... "I bet it would be good on pretzels." ... (breathe) ... "These pretzels are making me thirsty. Ha ha. I miss Kramer." ... (mini breath) ... "I heard that the puffy shirt is in the Smithsonian." ... (forget to breathe) ... "I ate crab won tons in the Washington, D.C. airport once."

I go from convening with the Universe ... to Nutella ... to Seinfeld ... to crab wontons in ten seconds flat.

Then I start over.

Which is fine.

Many people have difficulty meditating or want to give up on it because, honestly, it's not easy. This is mostly because we're not taught or trained in our western culture how to do it, nor do most of us have models for it, as you commonly would in other parts of the world.

For me, the idea of meditation goes back to the hippie couple down the street when I was a kid.

I pet sat for them once, and mostly what I remember about their house was that it smelled like incense and they kept a big ol' color copy of the *Kama Sutra* on the coffee table. He push-mowed their wild lawn in tiny, frayed cut-offs, and I'm pretty sure she breast-fed goats. They were meditators. This was my model of meditation. And at the time, my life revolved around watching *Dallas* and studying the JC Penney fall catalog for fashion trends that I'd never duplicate, so their spiritual, organic way of life was completely wasted on me.

Meditation is weird, I'm sure I murmured to myself later over my catalog, while sipping a Tab, snapping my gum, and circling a mauve argyle sweater.

These days, meditation has become much more common, and there's an army of celebrities touting its benefits, from David Lynch to Hugh Jackman to Katie Perry to Paul McCartney. It's thankfully, becoming a part of the western world ... not for religious purposes, but more for its mind and health benefits.

In a way, meditation is like learning a foreign language. It's something that just takes practice and repetition to get the groove of. When starting out, the three most important factors to remember are:

1. You can't get it wrong.
2. Approach it as fun, not a chore.
3. Find a quiet place.

You can meditate anywhere, but I find having a designated space helpful. I turned a closet into a meditation space for myself. I did this because my mind usually runs like a Super Bowl halftime show, and the closet gives me a dark, distraction-free place to slow down and unplug. I added some pillows, good smells, and warm, dim lighting for ambiance (those things aren't necessary, but anything that relaxes you is helpful) ... but again, like I said, your meditation place can be as simple as *anywhere* you are.

When first starting meditation, don't set your goal on having some psychedelic adventure or hearing the voice of Morgan Freeman. Rather, simply decide you're going to relax and treat yourself to an enjoyable mind break. In the same way your body enjoys a dip into a hot tub as a respite from an active day, you're going to dip your mind into a mental hot tub.

When meditating, you don't need to sit upright in a chair or cross-legged on the floor, just sit or lie down in any position that is comfortable. Also, you don't have to chant a mantra or "Oooooom" like they do in cartoons or sitcoms when they spoof someone meditating. *Ōm*, by the way, does have a meaning. It is the sound of a sacred spiritual symbol (it looks like a fancy number three to us) in Indian religions, mainly Hinduism, that signifies consciousness, or that which is everything. Indian practices often use *Ōm* during meditation, but you don't need to use it in yours, unless you want to.

When I sit down to meditate, I set the mood and get comfy in my closet. I then start taking lots of deep, long breaths and I observe how my body feels. I do a body scan from my toes to my forehead, clenching each of my muscle groups tight for a few seconds, and then releasing them as I work my way up. I go through this a few times until my muscles feel relaxed.

Go ahead and try it right now. I know you already are.

Once you've dipped your body into your mental hot tub, and you're feeling pretty free and easy, then ease your mind in. Let yourself feel a little hazy and focus on something neutral, like your natural breathing, an appliance humming (my dishwasher has a pleasant, steady chant to it; we meditate together), or even dim spa music.

With eyes closed, step out of your day and focus on being present in that moment. Sometimes as I sit, I envision an empty, quiet intersection in the middle of the night. Occasionally a thought car ("don't forget to buy Nutella") goes by. Just let it go, no big deal, and refocus on the emptiness. If you do this for a while, you'll likely notice your body and face start to feel heavy, your mind feels lighter, and you begin to feel a pleasant disconnect. (Sometimes you may even feel sleepy and doze off—go ahead and take a nap if you do. Naps are all good, too.)

The disconnect is the meditation sweet spot. It's your mind gently leaving your body and realigning with your non-physical soul … and it feels like hot tubbing in a resistance-free, unspoiled paradise.

Soak in it for as long as you can.

And don't worry if it takes a long time to get there, or if you *can't* get there.

Sometimes, I'm in the closet for fifteen minutes and only two of them are spent in that sweet spot *or* I never get there at all. Like I said, you can't get it wrong, and the good news is that even two minutes in the sweet spot, or fifteen minutes of pure, undisturbed relaxation is often still enough to you get back into alignment with Source.

The best part of meditation is how you feel when you come out of it.

When I come out of a meditation, I feel present and playful. It feels like my worry faucet has been completely shut off and my appreciation faucet has been fully turned on.

It's a gratifying little reunion with the Universe that leaves me feeling like pure love.

The insanely sharp, successful, and fit Jerry Seinfeld, who began practicing transcendental meditation in his college days, says he loves to share the benefits of meditation with anyone who will listen.

"Every person I meet now, I just feel like grabbing them by the lapels and saying, you gotta do this," he says.

"… because it's just a dumb way to live, not doing it. It's just dumb. Being a person is hard. You need a break folks, you need a break."

We do need breaks and meditation is one of the most natural ones we can take. Its benefits are obvious enough that I'd say it's absolutely worth anyone giving it a try.

So, consider this your simple, basic, Seinfeld-approved introduction to meditation.

Now grab your towel, find your hot tub … and you take it from here.

chapter five

***

enlightenment and potato salad

Let's dip our toes in some holy water and talk about religion, specifically Christianity, as it is the largest religion in the world.

As a spiritual path, most denominations of Christianity are based on the core belief that Jesus Christ was the only divine son of God and that he sacrificed himself to pay the debt for our sins, therefore allowing those who accept him as their savior to gain access to the Kingdom of Heaven.

For myself, though I was a once a whole-hearted believer of that Christian message, I find too much confusion in it (and less in other beliefs) for me to follow it exclusively now. If you are a full or partial believer in the Christian message, I respect that

that is your choice. To each his own. I understand why many people are faithful to it—not just because of the beliefs, but because we humans also enjoy participating in the traditions, community, and holidays that accompany it.

So, if Christianity is meaningful to you, I understand.

I would respectfully disagree with you, however, if you insist that it is the only path to God for everyone.

George Carlin nails my current view with this quip.

"Religion has actually convinced people that there's an invisible man living in the sky who watches everything you do, every minute of every day. And the invisible man has a special list of ten things he does not want you to do. And if you do any of these ten things, he has a special place, full of fire and smoke and burning and torture and anguish, where he will send you to live and suffer and burn and choke and scream and cry forever and ever 'til the end of time! But He loves you."

That's the confusion that I'm talking about.

It doesn't make sense to me to say,

"…God is love" (1 John 4:8) and beautifully define love as, "Love is patient, love is kind. It does not envy, it does not boast, it is not proud. It does not dishonor others, it is not self-seeking, it is not easily angered, it keeps no record of wrongs. Love does not delight in evil but rejoices with the truth. It always protects, always trusts, always hopes, always perseveres. Love never fails." (1 Corinthians 13: 4-8)

… but then also preach that God is a judgmental God, who may condemn you to a torturous, eternal damnation if you don't choose him.

If God is love, he sounds anything *but* judgmental.

That line, "…it keeps no records of wrongs," is also pivotal for me when it comes to believing that mankind needs a savior to pay the debt for their sins. If "God is love," and love "keeps no record of wrongs" … isn't that saying that there is *no* debt to pay for our sins?

Again, it doesn't make sense to me.

Also, the original meaning of sin meant "misses the target" or "off the mark," like in archery. It's a neutral term. We all sin, we miss the mark at times, we're human—it's ok; that's what apologies and forgiveness are for. But somewhere along the way, sin got eternal worthiness attached to it and it became *bad bad bad* to miss the mark, not just human. Man started attaching shame and condemnation to missing the mark, which makes me wonder if our egos didn't create a savior figure to set things right with themselves and God (a God that was never judging sin in the first place).

I'm not saying Jesus didn't exist. I absolutely believe that he did. I think the parables are nuggets of gold to live by, and if there was a church that focused solely on the significance of his life and teachings, rather than his death, I'd be there. I love Jesus. But I'm not convinced that the Bible's interpretation of his life is all *fact*.

I agree with the British-American philosopher Alan Watts, who once said, "I do believe … that there is a sense in which the Bible is divinely inspired, but I mean by inspiration something utterly different from dictation, receiving a dictated message from an omniscient authority."

I, too, believe there's divine inspiration in the Bible. But it was still recorded and assembled by man, a long time ago, in a completely different time and culture, so I don't believe it's logical to try to interpret the Bible literally. Besides the fact that it's meanings and words have likely been mistranslated and influenced by man's ego for millennia, I also ask myself, *why* try to make sense of something so old when there's modern spiritual teachings to consider, which offer more clarity for this time in our existence?

Regardless of where you stand in your beliefs—with Jesus the Savior, Jesus the teacher, or no Jesus at all—again, to each his own. We all, thankfully, have free will to choose. And whether any beliefs are hurting or helping mankind only depends on how they're used. As a personal spiritual practice, any belief can be used as a model for loving ourselves and others, *or* it can be used as a mass egoic fear vehicle to control and disempower others.

And I think that's where the other element of religion comes into consideration. Besides just the fundamental *beliefs*, there's the man-made *institutions* of religions at play, and I think it's important to differentiate the two.

I've received messages from many readers who once felt lost in their spiritual beliefs because, as children, they suffered at the hands of the institution of religion. They had guilt, fear, and radical discipline forced on them by adults ... all in the name of *a loving God*.

Somewhere along the way, the beliefs got grossly distorted by the institution.

The beliefs of most religions are based on the core teachings of some enlightened master.

It starts out simple. A teacher has a top-of-the-ladder experience of connecting to Source energy, they begin to teach others what they know, and a community begins to form around them and their teachings.

Eventually, the teacher dies, the community becomes a religion, and egoic man is now at the helm. More time goes on, and the teachings have become part of a religious institution, run by men and women who add their own interpretations and practices to the original message (case in point: there are thousands of denominations and sects, each with different messages of "practice this, eat this, wear this" in *all* religions, worldwide), until the religion has become more like a culture, often far removed from the enlightened teacher's original message.

I don't think that it's necessarily wrong or right that this happens, it just does. Institutions need structure; and the more egos get involved in anything, the more distorted and convoluted even the best intentions can get.

Regardless of the belief, I think all religions and churches, even hippie ones, can be assets or obstacles to our personal growth. Sharing our spiritual thoughts and experiences with a community of like-minded people can be comforting and insightful, but at the same time, we can easily get side-tracked from a personal connection to Source by thinking that the community is the core of our strength and identity, rather than what's inside us.

I think we get *much* too caught up in the social aspect of it these days.

Congregating with others around potato salad isn't the path to Source. Personal inner solitude is the path to Source.

The great irony in history is that most every major religion was formed around the master teachings of someone that found enlightenment in solitude, not in a group setting. Moses went up the mountain, Jesus wandered the desert, Mohammed was in a cave, Lao Tzu was on a long journey, and the Buddha was under a bodhi tree. Enlightenment didn't happen for any of them at a Sunday morning sermon, in a religious middle school classroom, or at a singles bowling night.

I think we should keep that in mind a little more ... true enlightenment happens in solitude.

So, that's my two bits of frankincense and myrrh on Christianity and religion in general, based on my own experience. Religion is helpful and it's harmful. It brings us connection with each other, but may be unintentionally distracting and disconnecting us from a personal connection to Source by doing so.

Just like spirituality, there's an enormous spectrum to it, from the beliefs, to the institutions, and more.

It's a big, sticky subject.

What I do know is, that neither you nor I require being in a church or aligning with any one religion to have access to God. Nor are we under any obligation to take any religion as all or nothing, because no one faith has the universal monopoly on the truth. I am the only one who can decide my own spiritual truths, as are you. It's only controlling egos that ever insists otherwise.

Maybe someday, as our planet continues to awaken, we'll each be more inclined to lay down our rigidity, think more independently, and declare to our fellow man, as the poet John Keats penned centuries ago, that "Love is my religion."

chapter six

***

i forsee a slurpee ...

Astrology, psychics, and tarot ... are they real?

Astrology: Is it relevant or real?

I don't think so, for a couple of reasons.

First, we only ever live in the present, so why my birth date should affect what's happening to me my *entire* life strikes me immediately as irrelevant. It's just the calendar date that I took my first breath, in my little balloon body, with my *"Hello, my name is Julie Rasmussen"* name tag on it.

I moved on from that day years ago, and I think it is undoubtedly my present-day experiences and vibration, and not what sign I was born under, that's influencing my current life path.

Secondly, I've never had a personal *Shazam!* moment

regarding astrology that has convinced me that it's valid or valuable.

Horoscopes can seem eerily spot-on at times, I won't deny that, but I won't attribute it to someone having the ability to make accurate, personal predictions for an enormous collective of people (there's roughly 650 million people *per* astrological sign walking the earth every day) based on the alignment of stars and planets.

When a horoscope seems relevant, it's likely three other things are happening:

1. The predictions are so vague that they can apply to anybody about anything.

2. It's the Law of Attraction at work. You read a horoscope about how "You'll be meeting your new lover in an unexpected place" ... while you were still thinking about the hot dude or chick you saw over by the Slurpee machine while standing in line at 7-11 that morning. The psychic didn't make some fantastical prediction; you just attracted and read that horoscope that day because the Law of Attraction brought those similar thoughts together.

3. The ever-present power of suggestion (which is not neither good or bad) is influencing you to seek truth in the prediction, i.e. you're going to start hanging out in that 7-11 more, *expecting* to find your Slurpee-sucking new lover ... and the prediction (per suggestion) may actually come true.

So, while astrology may feel like truth at times, I think there are other explanations and contributing factors making it so. Personally, I think astrology is far too general and impersonal to be taken seriously or to guide one's life by.

It's a left swipe for me.

Psychics and Tarot readers: Are they are real?

Yes, I think so. But like auto mechanics, not all are good or honest.

Generally, psychics are people who can see things on your path or in your future, based on where you are vibrationally that day. And while science has no proof for psychic abilities (no big whoop—science has no proof for many spiritual things), I have witnessed psychics whom I genuinely believe can tune themselves to non-physical frequencies and broadcast back what they're receiving ... yes, sometimes even relaying future events.

I think it can be done.

So yes, psychic *abilities* are real in my opinion.

But not all *psychics* are real.

And paying repeatedly for a psychic to read your future is an entirely different crystal ball.

I've only been to one psychic, one time, and it was just enough to convince me that the ability exists and to leave it at that. She was accurate, sincere, and did it for people whom she thought it would help. She was the good and honest type of psychic mechanic. There are many like this.

Alex tried a psychic once out of his own curiosity and walked out, minus fifty dollars later, with a jumbled, verbal cauldron of predictions related to turtles, the color purple, Iceland, dragon flies, and Uranus ... none of which ever came true. It was utter, useless nonsense. That was the bad and dishonest type of psychic mechanic. There are plenty of them, as well.

Tarot readers are similar to psychics in that they can give you information about your path.

Tarot is when someone has you pick cards from a special Tarot deck and then they read to you what the cards mean. Versus a psychic doing all the work, the Tarot reader is only interpreting the cards that you have chosen.

Tarot makes some sense to me because I am contributing to what's happening by pulling the cards. But again, the Law of Attraction may just be attracting me to pull cards that relate to hot dudes in 7-11 because that's what's on my mind. So bear in mind, the cards you pull and the interpretation you receive from them are just the product of what's in your vibe *that* day—it doesn't mean it's some pre-determined destiny.

An honest psychic or tarot reader should always remind you that they're just a middleman between you and Source and that your readings can change from day to day. A good one won't keep your credit card on file or manipulate you into feeling like you need to come back for more.

In summary, if there's one universal truth in spirituality, I'd say it's this ... it's about going *inside* yourself for truth and answers. And all of these things are about going *outside* of yourself.

That being said, I suggest taking your fifty dollars to go buy some candles and groovy pillows, and make a meditation space for yourself instead. Eliminate the middleman and go straight to Source yourself. Get into alignment with feeling great; and rather than obsessing over predictions, kick back and allow the manifestations of your life to surprise and delight you as they unfold.

(And save a little cash for Slurpees with your new lover.)

chapter seven

***

petey, the chicken killer

Resistance feels like being lost in the Land of Negativity. Everyone there just schleps around unproductively, arguing for their limitations, blaming others, and bitching about how unfair life is. And it's twice as frustrating when you're awakened enough that you know you don't want to be there, but you can't seem to get out.

I went through resistance when I first started writing about spirituality. As I kept moving up the ladder, following my desire to write about it, my ego would hold me back for weeks with encouraging messages, like,

"People are going to call you fucking crazy!"

Messages that were always negative, dooms day declarations. Egos are the motivational speakers from hell.

My true self always knew that those thoughts weren't real,

but my ego was clinging for control. And hence, a painful, high noon stand-off of resistance would ensue.

Meditation is the surest way to clear resistance—just shut all thinking down, right?

Absolutely.

And if you can do it, great!

But unfortunately, for many people (including me) it's nearly impossible to meditate when you're deep in the Land of Negativity. It's not like there's relaxing classes on it there, or that anyone would go even if there was. (sidebar: I met myself in a mediation class once. No, not figuratively, I mean literally. There was a woman named Julie Rasmussen in the class with me.)

I think when resistance is just too strong, the only thing to do is accept that you feel bottom-rung yucky (accepting it will, thankfully, immediately lessen some of it), get some sleep, and hope that tomorrow you'll feel like crawling out from under your bed.

Sit with the frustration, lean into it, and be patient.

It will run its course.

My own resistance was annoying. When meditation was difficult, taking naps, or listening to calming music or positive talks from my favorite teachers, helped release some of it.

Crying and venting also releases resistance, so weeping hysterically while eating cheese flavored popcorn and watching *Brokeback Mountain* also helped. As did aggressively shoving shopping carts into cart corrals from 200 yards across parking lots, whenever possible.

Alcohol is a temporary resistance reducer, as well.

Now, I'm *absolutely not* endorsing alcohol as a regular, go-to resistance reducer, because it's only ever a temporary fix (it's a band-aid on an open wound), but I'm being honest, and I won't shame anyone who has occasionally turned to it during shit times, because I know I have. While I rarely drink these days, I purposely opened a bottle of Sour Grapes Winery *I Haven't Showered in Three Days Merlot* for temporary relief during some hard times in the past.

I call alcohol a resistance reducer, because I know it had that effect on me, but allowing it to reduce resistance can go too far.

Case in point: Petey the dachshund.

The Santa Fe (New Mexico) Brewing Company has a beer called "Chicken Killer." The story behind its name, as I learned on their brewery tour, is that Petey was a local, mild-mannered dachshund in the small, rural town where they test their beers.

One day after working on a new brew, the leftover sediment was poured in the far corner of an empty field. As the story goes, Petey found and consumed the alcohol sediment ... and then went on a primal rampage, chasing down and killing thirteen chickens around town.

I asked the brewery tour guide if Petey was ok afterwards, and he said, "Yes, he was fine."

I then asked if Petey had any memory of, or visible remorse for, his actions.

The guide said, "I don't know. He didn't say."

So, based on my poorly researched and very non-scientific study of Petey "The Chicken Killer" dachshund, I conclude that it's probably best to limit your use of alcohol as a resistance reducer, and thus avoid becoming a cautionary tale of unpredictability on a beer tour someday.

Eliminating things, not just adding things to my life, also helped with progressing through resistance. I stayed away from things that feed the ego (I was going to starve my ego out if I couldn't make her leave!). Anything that feeds fear is feeding the ego, so I took a long hiatus from social media and the news. I also eliminated *all* commercials, with their constant fear and lack messages, from my mental diet.

Deliberately choosing what you expose your mind to is a big step up the enlightenment ladder. It's not irresponsible to limit your news intake for your own well-being, and don't apologize for it—this is *your* life. As a collective, we probably wouldn't have so much fear-based news if we all paid more attention to our own well-being, and less to the news anyway.

My favorite, and the surest way to raise my vibe, is to get into nature. It is the universe in its purest, most naked form, and it can help cure what ails you, if you let it.

"I'd rather be in the mountains thinking of God, than in church thinking about the mountains," said author and naturalist John Muir.

Go kiss a pinecone, rub some dirt in your hands, and purposely listen to the birds. Focus on the sky and the grass and temporarily let all the bullshit go.

Return to the oneness of it all, and remember who you really are … part of a fantastic universe of balance and beauty.

My last advice is this, it's impossible to feel awful and feel appreciation at the same time, so count your blessings, even if they feel small.

Managing my resistance got much easier with time. Resistance simply means that your soul is expanding, which is good news. Don't lose sight of that.

Author Creig Crippen offers us this supportive, powerful reminder for you to copy and keep next to you, under your bed, if needed ...

"Have you ever thought to yourself, 'I think I might be going a little crazy,' but then you remember that you're really just an awakened, loving, kickass warrior, hell bent on changing the world, and you refuse to accept the negative vibrations, and the fear and the hate and the illusion of separation, and you remember that there are many others just like you, that stand with you, the alchemists, the conscious warriors, the rule breakers, the lovers of life, the ones that are determined to lift each other up and to ensure that love wins, the ones that are just crazy enough to get the job done, and then you remember that you're not crazy at all and you're not alone, you're just awake?

Yep, me too. You're good.

Keep going."

chapter eight

***

those things we do

I have porn on my mind, and it started with a sermon.

It was one I heard years ago at a local church.

Now this is where I may be stepping into uncomfortable territory for some of you with my opinions *(like I didn't already do that when I said, "let's put the fun back in funeral"),* but let's throw pornography, and all our other vices, across the kitchen table for discussion.

I remember the pastor who gave the sermon had a firm perspective that pornography destroys relationships (he was even wearing a tee-shirt that said, "Porn Kills Love").

He presented a long list of statistics on how booming and profitable (we're talking billions) the porn industry is, generating more money than a handful of major U.S. companies combined. He followed that with some statistics on the high percentage of people who admit to watching porn. He then told the congregation that "We need to extradite sin from our lives," (which I'm pretty sure is only possible *by dying*) and wrapped things up with "Repent, yadda, yadda, Jesus saves, yadda yadda, coffee and donuts in the lobby. Go Broncos."

Now my three main takeaways from that message were this:

1. Is occasionally watching porn something that requires "admitting" to?

2. Did he make that shirt?

3. Boy, this guy sure knows a lot about porn.

While I respect this pastor's good intentions, I don't share his perspective or his logic.

Pornography and our other vices *aren't* what destroy relationships.

Addictions are what destroy relationships.

And the root of addiction is shame and pain.

Pornography, and those other things we do—excessive use of alcohol, food, social media, pot, work, religion, gambling, shopping, sex, and gaming (I'm not talking about predatory, illegal, or abusive things here, just vices)—are outlets and coping mechanisms that manifest while trying to medicate or avoid, some deeper problem in one's life.

These vices are not the *cause* of a problem ... they're the *effect* of a problem.

And if the root of an addiction or coping is a deep wound festering in someone's life, should we really be shaming one other and ourselves about it? Isn't preaching blind restraint just making it worse by adding *more* shame on someone who's already struggling to find relief from their pain? Wouldn't it be more Buddha-like and Christ-like to be understanding toward each other's wounds and addictions, instead of judgmental?

If a vice isn't illegal or endangering anyone else, show some compassion. Respect the person's soul. Be encouraging without enabling. I know it's not easy, but try taking yourself out of the equation for a while and just be a neutral observer. Don't feed both egos more energy by nagging and obsessing about what it's doing to *you* ... because it's not about you, it's about them.

The heart of the matter is that people only change when they are ready and willing to change, and no one should need to change for *you* to feel secure and happy. That weight is on you, not them. You can't force change on someone else (there's no Law of Assertion, only a Law of Attraction), but you can influence them with your own behavior ... *if* the change that you represent is what they're seeking.

So, if you don't like your partner's porn addiction, then stop giving constant attention to your partner's porn addiction. Give them some space, offer love, and go be a porn-free confident person yourself and see what happens. Eventually, either they'll join you ... or you'll vibrate out of each other's lives.

Either way, it will be for the better.

I think that most vices and addictions originate from believing the illusion that we are separate from Source.

Forgetting who we really are is painful.

Believing we are disconnected from unconditional love, that we are stuck in our past traumas, and that we are constantly being judged can smother even the strongest and sweetest of people under the fear cloud.

Though it's not a simple or quick-fix journey, I do believe that a return, or awakening, to our true soul nature is the ultimate answer to any wound or problem. Even if you've had massive trauma, Source is bigger than it.

Reconnecting to unconditional love can heal any wound we have. And when we stop hurting, we stop coping, and our need for vices slowly dissipates.

So, I suppose, from my paper pulpit here, I would teach it the opposite way.

Porn doesn't kill love ... but the power of love *could* kill a porn addiction ... *and all our other problems.*

chapter nine

***

james bond and salsa recipes

It's not easy to admit that you're in a serious, committed relationship with Source energy in our modern world.

I had a lot of resistance to communicating the shift in my spiritual understanding to others in the beginning, mostly because I was afraid of what they would think of me. I wasn't looking forward to the quizzical, confused looks that I anticipated staring back at me while trying to explain all this.

I expected and feared that I wouldn't fit into my old social circles anymore once I came out of the closet about my awakening. It was a paradox, I didn't want to let go of those old circles (and feel alone), yet I also knew that I had changed ... and I didn't particularly want to stay in them either.

Let's just say, once you've had that experience that bursts you through the insanity of the egoic fear cloud and awakens you to the love and intelligence of the limitless cosmos ... that it's hard to go back to listening to friends and family talk about how their HOA is on their ass about their garbage cans.

Conversations about HOAs, sports, shopping, or salsa recipes, that I would have gladly participated in in the past, became so incredibly mundane and irritating to me that I had to just retreat from the world for a while.

And I felt guilty as hell about it.

I was distancing myself from family and friends—some that I had known for decades, through no fault of their own. They hadn't done anything wrong; I just couldn't relate to them anymore. While I cared about them, I no longer cared about what they cared about.

I did try talking to some of these people about my awakening experience, and it was a gamechanger/ender for a few. Some looked at me with concern, like I was on drugs or in a cult, and others just quickly disappeared on me all together.

"Goodbye! I don't blame you! This sounds crazy! I'd run, too!" I yelled at the back of their heads, wishing them well, as they scurried away.

I spent a lot of time alone, which truthfully, was what I needed and what I enjoyed. Alone time helped me find clarity in my own experience without the distraction of other people's opinions. Enlightenment happens in solitude, as I said earlier.

Sometimes, you just need to let go of what others think and go your own way.

Like George Lazenby.

George Lazenby is an Australian film actor and former model. He is best known for having played British secret agent James Bond in the film *On Her Majesty's Secret Service* (1969). At age 29, he was the youngest actor to have portrayed Bond and he's the only Bond actor to have received a Golden Globe nomination.

According to a 2017 documentary entitled *Becoming Bond*, George was a handsome car salesman and mechanic, who stumbled into modeling and acting. He admittedly fabricated his acting experience to get the role of James Bond, replacing Sean Connery, the original Bond.

He made *On Her Majesty's Secret Service,* which was so well-received that he was offered a contract for six more Bond films with a one-million-dollar bonus … which he turned down.

While the movie was being publicized and promoted, he grew a beard and dressed as he pleased, which infuriated the movie's executives, because they wanted him to *be* James Bond at all times.

He walked away because he didn't like them telling him how to look and act off-screen.

He wasn't James Bond.

James Bond was fiction.

He was George Lazenby.

So, he quit (and took a mountain of grief for it in the press). He went on to do a few other movie roles, pursue hobbies and businesses, have a family, and live a good life.

I find this such an incredible story of someone knowing who they are.

"You can defy what is expected of you and write your own

story," George said later in life, while wisely adding from his own experience, "I lived my life the way I wanted to. The best thing you can do is to know yourself."

Eventually, as I came to know myself better, I stopped trying to hold on to what no longer served me, and I let go of old relationships, without guilt.

And as old friends left, new ones came along. And instead of having a wide circle of acquaintances, as I had once had, I found myself content with a much smaller group of relatable, intimate friends. I traded a hundred pennies for four quarters, I like to say.

Brianna Wiest, American writer, speaker, and the author of *101 Essays That Will Change the Way You Think* says this on the subject, "Your new life is going to cost you your old one. It's going to cost you your comfort zone and your sense of direction. It's going to cost you relationships and friends. It's going to cost you being liked and understood. But it doesn't matter. Because the people who are meant for you are going to meet you on the other side. And you're going to build a new comfort zone around the things that move you forward. And instead of liked, you're going to be loved. Instead of understood, you're going to be seen.

All you're going to lose is what was built for a person you no longer are. Let it go."

chapter ten

***

#cleavageandcobbsalads

It's a worthwhile question to ask these days. Is social media making us better or worse people?

And just like anything else, including religion as I discussed earlier, it all depends on how it's used. It's the intention of the person behind the tool that matters. And social media is the most powerful communication tool in human history, so it has a lot of influence, for better *and* for worse.

It's the world's largest bulletin board. It lets us share our ideas, common interests, events, and adorable cat videos with one another instantly. And for that, I praise and appreciate it.

It's also a narcissistic brag board full of superficiality, comparison, unnecessary cleavage, and boring-ass Cobb salads. And for that, I cringe at it.

Looking back, social media started out as a hobby for me. When it first came out, it was a way to catch up with people that I wouldn't have heard from otherwise. I eased myself in, posting funny anecdotes and pictures, only to people that I knew.

It was a fun, harmless novelty.

Fast-forward five years later, and I'm now posting perfect-looking pictures of myself to total strangers of how jolly and fascinating my life is because I'm unknowingly addicted to the "hit" of getting likes.

Now, *giving* likes is not really a bad thing. People mean well by liking something.

A Psychology Today blog by Liraz Mrgalit, Phd, says this about likes, "From the sender's perspective, sending a like can have the same effect as smiling or saying a kind word to someone. It is basically a really easy, low-cost way to communicate positive feedback."

Ok, fair enough, the problem isn't in *giving* likes on social media. The problem becomes our unhealthy desire to *receive* them. That's when social media goes from a brilliant communication medium ... to a dumpster fire ego feed.

From my own experience, I can tell you I used social media the most in life when I had a career that had me moving in circles with local celebrities. I was bringing in the love like an easy prom queen because I'd post pictures of me with notable people, gushing about how "proud and blessed I was" ... instead of just flat-out saying, "Blah, blah, blah, I'm bragging because my ego could use your approval." #blah #needy

Oh, I looked flawless and successful in those pics (Because

why ever post a bad picture of yourself, am I right?), but I can tell you that it was also the loneliest time in my life, and that's why I used social media the most. I was unconsciously trolling for likes because I simply lacked connection to anything deeper. I was filling emotional voids through other people acknowledging me. And yes, the likes and comments felt satisfying for a while, but it was always a temporary, impersonal substitute for meaningful connection.

On the scale of meaningful connections, alignment with Source comes in first, like an endless ocean of love.

It's followed by a tranquil mountain lake of good friends, family, and love relationships.

Social media brings up the rear ... like an inflatable swimming pool from K-mart.

It's still water to splash in, but it's a shallow, plastic pool.

It's a convenient place to find connection, that, by design, thrives on short, surface level connections. And there's no problem with all that, so long as you understand it and don't attach your self-worth to the shallow, plastic pool.

Besides it being an easy ego trap, I see social media's other problematic negative in that it robs us of being satisfied with the present moment. As soon as we post something, we've left the present and are now in two places at once—half checking our phones for other people's reactions—and half invested in listening to the Phish concert happening right in front of us.

We're missing *so much* of what we came for when we post about it.

So, as far as social media destroying mankind, well, I don't think that's going to happen, so long as we keep *ourselves* in check. It's up to you to decide if it makes your life better or worse.

Maybe it wouldn't hurt for us all to ask ourselves, however, before the next time we're tempted to post …

"Am I losing being present by posting this?"

And *"Will the world really miss this picture of me, my cleavage, and my Cobb salad … or will I miss their approval?"*

And most importantly, *"Is this connection satisfying, or am I seeking something deeper?"*

These days, I've detoxed from the need for likes, and I use social media in moderation. I've found my harmony with the tool, vowing to never turn my self-worth over to it, or anything else, again … and I wish you the same.

So, while social media can conveniently fill some needs, reconnecting to Source, yourself, and personal relationships, can lovingly and permanently, fill them much better.

I guess, happily, we will have to meet in person if you're to ever meet me, my cleavage, or my Cobb salad.

#putdownthephonephishison

chapter eleven

***

meat me in yoga class ... or not

There's two common assumptions that many people have about being a spiritual or awkened person.

1. It requires being vegan or vegetarian.
2. It requires doing yoga.

Now, I'm all for being vegan or vegetarian if it makes someone feel healthier, or because they personally don't want to eat animals or use animal products for ethical reasons. Go for it. I even had a time period when I first went through awakening that eating meat, physically and emotionally, nauseated me. I get it, and your feelings are legitimate to you, so eat as you please.

For me, though, those feelings eventually passed, and I now think it is entirely possible to greatly respect animals *and* eat them, too.

I do believe that animals feel suffering and stress and should be treated humanely. I believe that loading our meat and dairy products with artificial chemicals is not best . I also believe that methane gas from cow farts is contributing to a hole in the ozone. That's not bullshit.

But I do think when we start humanizing animal emotions too much, that things can get, well, a little bullshitty.

My theory on why we humanize animals stems, in part, from the endless stories portraying animals with human emotions (anthropomorphism) that we are exposed to in childhood. When you think of most fairy tales, kids' movies, or children's books, they're packed with animals having human-like qualities and intentions.

I remember feeling so conflicted as a kid after seeing *Charlotte's Web*.

I mean, that story's message is essentially:

Cute pig = good. Bacon = bad.

So as a gentle grade-schooler, I felt like I should absolutely side with cute pig. But the truth was, though I liked Wilbur (I mean, what's not to like about his pink, squishy body, and child-like demeanor?) ... I *still* wanted to eat bacon on Saturday mornings while watching cartoons (ironically enough, while probably watching Porky Pig).

A childhood of the Pink Panther, Alf, and Miss. Piggy, weirdly taught me that animals (ok, Alf was an alien, but he looks like an animal) must think like me.

But animals *don't* think like humans, or they wouldn't be out there in the wind and rain rolling in their own feces.

I don't think the cows that I pass in fields as I drive across the plains are saying to themselves, *"I'm dyyyyyyying,"* nor are they making bucket lists ...

"I never told Margaret that I loved her. I never learned to surf. I never backpacked through Europe."

If they thought like humans, they would be organizing themselves to scale barbed wire fences in the middle of the night, walk single file down the interstate to the nearest town, get a motel room, and call PETA.

But they don't do that, because, again ... they're cows.

And I'm no expert, but logically, if we didn't use cows, pigs, and chickens for products, wouldn't they go extinct? We couldn't de-domesticate them (Chicken hunting season? Trophy chickens?) and they'd be impractical pets for most people.

So, couldn't not eating them to save them, in the end, potentially kill them all off anyway and/or massively disrupt the food chain, nature, and a lot of economics?

From my perspective, *everything* that has life, repeatedly and eternally, originates and returns to Source energy—even balloon animals get the welcome home party for the soul and come back again. So, to me, the perfect, simple consciousness of a cow doesn't know or care that it comes into its body to be food or product. It doesn't aspire for more than to just "be." "Being" is its repeating life function, like going to work every day is for most of us humans.

I think it's just our egos, projecting our human emotions onto animals, that see things otherwise.

I am positive Miss. Piggy would agree with me on this.

Vegans and vegetarians do help cut down on cow farts and

are contributing to the human collective by encouraging local, ethical farming practices.

Meat eaters give animals value and provide employment to their fellow man by doing so. There's a positive contribution to the human collective in that, as well.

So, to meat or not to meat? It really doesn't matter.

Just keep your fancy hamburgers and boring-ass Cobb salads off social media, Ok?

The second assumption that I had to clear up for myself is that being a spiritual person means I'm supposed to be into yoga.

Yoga has a long, rich tradition with spirituality and though I've tried it a few times I can't say I'm a regular, for no particular reason. From my experience, it can be useful and enjoyable, but it's not essential to a spiritual practice. I own yoga pants, and they've been to my local donut shop way more times than they've been to a yoga class. In fact, I've decided to drop any yoga reference in their name altogether, and re-name them a more honest and accurate, pants-I-wear-when-I-don't-want-to-wear-regular-pants-to-the-donut-shop-pants. (sidebar: I dreamed once that I opened a donut shop, and with superb ridiculousness named it "Hole Foods.")

While I think it's beneficial for the body and mind, yoga still feels like an activity that I don't make time for, like water polo. That may likely change someday, but for now I'm just as content to take a nice long walk to clear my mind and move my body.

So, my point here isn't that being healthy is bad. *Of course* it's not bad. My point is that always being a perfect eater and physically fit isn't a requirement of a spiritual life. Those things don't make you spiritual, nor do you need them to be spiritual.

Hell, I see signs and synchronicities all day long, and I write books on these airy-fairy loads of crap ... and I had a Diet Coke and a few Oreos for breakfast the other day.

Life isn't a competition of looking more fit, more spiritual, or happier than thou. There are no congratulatory plaques or awards handed out when we die for "Most Consecutive Hot Yoga Days," or for "Looking Good for Your Age." (What's really so wrong with looking like shit for your age, so long as you have inner peace and know who you are?). Gluten-free pasta won't fix childhood trauma, six-pack abs aren't the cure for life-long insecurities (nor, unfortunately, are spray tans and super white teeth—I know, I tried).

Nothing outside of you will get you out of the fear cloud.

Only your mind can do that.

If you truly want a healthy body, start at the core, by making a healthy *mind* your priority. Recognize your ego, address your emotional blockages (that likely contributed to your unhealthy patterns or unfit body in the first place), and take accountability for your inner peace first. Try starting on the inside and working your way out, not the other way around.

Let your body follow your untroubled mind to the gym ... or the donut shop.

That's how you'll find the permanent, *real* results you're looking for.

chapter twelve

***

assholes, creeps, and dipshits

You've driven next to them, you've roomed with them, you've dated them, you've even married them. You grew up with them, you've worked for them, and you've waited on them.

They're the narcissists, the middle-finger wavers, the line cutters, the ghosters, the blamers, the cheaters, and the cheapskates.

They're the curmudgeon who snapped a dollar bill in Alex's face before, slowly and with unnecessary drama, putting it in the tip jar and sneering …

"It could have been a ten."

(Right, Ebenezer, like you've ever tipped a ten *in your life*.)

They're the SUV-driving Medusa in my rear-view mirror that's having a flailing, emotional seizure and honking at me for stopping at an intersection … to let a pedestrian, who had the right-of-way, cross.

And they're the pervy turd who sent an unsolicited, undesired, bizarrely holding a can of *Glade* air freshener next to his penis, dick pic.

They're assholes, creeps, and dipshits.

They're everywhere. And being a spiritual person doesn't mean you don't see their selfish, insensitive behavior or want to shoot them in the throat with poisoned blow darts.

So, what do we do about the assholes, creeps, and dipshits in our lives?

Well first, we understand that they're emotionally broken people. Somewhere along their life path, they likely endured abuse or trauma that caused them to feel insecure and powerless. So now they feed on power they take from others, often by purposely trying to make others feel uncomfortable, stupid, or worthless.

Sadly, they feel bigger and stronger when they make us feel small and weak.

Broken people are as old as time and will always exist. History will continue to be filled with assholes, creeps, and dipshits, so unfortunately, inviting them all on a cruise and leaving them at sea or lobotomizing them, are not viable, long-term solutions.

No, our only solution is to take the reins of our own emotional responses to them. Recognize that, as Eleanor Roosevelt once said, "No one can make you feel inferior without your consent."

Don't let them get your goat, become the ungettable goat.

Accept that while their lousy behavior *is* out of your control, how you *react* to it isn't.

So, let's begin by addressing where our negative emotions surrounding assholes, creeps, and dipshits are really coming from.

"Obviously, from their rotten, arrogant, stick-up-their-furry-monkey-ass, selfish behavior!" the ego stands and bellows.

Yes, their behavior is definitely the shit we can't stand, and while it can be a catalyst for our negative emotions, the true source of our discomfort goes deeper.

Sorry, ego. Go sit down.

The true source of our negative emotions is coming from within, from, for even a second, *believing* that we are small, stupid, or worthless. We hurt because we've let some toxic poop shooter tell us who we are, which puts us in conflict with our true selves who know we're *none* of those things.

Source energy is pure, unconditional love, therefore *I* am pure, unconditional love. Everyone's true nature is Buddha-like and Christ-like consciousness, and it painfully conflicts with our very nature to ever believe less than that about ourselves.

And to take it to a level deeper, our negative emotions are also coming from not just (even temporarily) judging ourselves incorrectly, but also from judging *the other*. They, too, at their core, are Source energy. So, to hate them also feels wrong.

It's like hating love.

It's soooo hard to admit, but we should actually *thank* assholes, creeps, and dipshits for helping for us remember who we really are. The negative emotions they spark in us are an indicator that we're out of alignment with the Source inside. The difficult other is often directing you back to your true self by being *as difficult as possible* because every negative emotion they spur in you is pushing you to seek relief in a higher, kinder, Source perspective.

If you accept them as providing an opportunity to come into alignment with your true self, rather than just being stinky, offensive burdens, strangely enough, assholes, creeps, and dipshits can serve us well.

If there's one worthwhile goal to set in life, it should be to achieve consistent happiness regardless of *anybody else's* behavior. And I think it can be done by mastering the practice of taking responsibility for how you feel, and by practicing "killing 'em with kindness" towards others.

All it requires is to quit listening to the ego's instinct to immediately blame others for our negative emotions, and to go within. Understand the other's broken behavior (important note: I'm not saying *like* their behavior, I'm just saying try *understanding* it), and just let it go.

Or in the flawlessly simple words of the late spiritual author and teacher, Dr. Wayne Dwyer, "When given the choice between being right or being kind, choose kind."

Remember our inner Christ/Buddha-like consciousness and practice patience and love from a higher perspective as much as possible ... not because it's the right or required thing to do, but because *it just feels better.*

In his book, *The Path to Tranquility*, the Dalai Lama XIV says, "It would be much more constructive if people tried to understand their supposed enemies. Learning to forgive is much more useful than merely picking up a stone and throwing it at the object of one's anger, the more so when the provocation is extreme. For it is under the greatest adversity that there exists the greatest potential for doing good, both for oneself and others."

So, the next time some obnoxious fart nozzle with a *"Fuck Your Feelings!"* bumper sticker passes you in the right-hand lane and leaves you in a cloud of black exhaust, calmly put down your rocks and blow darts, smile, and thank them for helping remind you who you really are.

Take the high road. It always leads home.

chapter thirteen

***

ned

I do most of my writing while lying in bed. A lot of deep thoughts and good jokes have come to me over the years while typing away on top of my covers, with a cat covered in sticky notes and my souvenir Graceland coffee mug, next to me.

Over time, I've developed a unique, personal bond with my mattress while I'm writing. So much so that I decided to give it a name a few years ago, "Ned."

When I'm ready to get into writing mode, I've tried sitting at a desk, I've tried reclining on the couch, and I've tried going to a local coffee shop ... but to no avail.

I always go back to reliable, soft yet firm, Ned.

Now, while this may sound strange to some, I come from a

family of people who name things all the time, so this is nothing new to me.

My sister, Carrie, planted some pear trees in her yard this year and named them Shirley Jones and David Cassidy (Google *The Partridge Family* if you're lost on this one).

My printer/copier's name is the Devil's Anus, my remote's name is Ramon, my aloe plant's name is Vera, and I will never have an herb garden without Rosemary Clooney and Phyllis Diller.

This is what we do in my family.

Now, I think part of why we do this is because we're using that personalization as a placebo, thinking it will somehow help our relationship with, or the performance of, whatever we've named (with the exception of my printer/copier, who's name simply reflects the *dark, evil piece of shit* that it is).

Which brings me to our next subject, spiritual accoutrements: crystals and sage.

Crystals are big business in the world of spirituality. Enter a spirituality bookstore and you'll find a crystal to help cure most every emotional and physical ailment you have. And while I do believe that everything is energy, I don't jibe with the idea that that sleeping with rocks all over my body can relieve my stress or backache, just through power of *the stones*.

What I do jibe with, however, is that if I *believe* the stones will help, then they most likely will.

And there's nothing wrong with that.

Placebos are not a bad thing at all, they're a helpful gateway to healing ourselves. Many people have been healed over the years with placebos, and the healing *is what* matters.

If you have hope or a belief that a certain stone will help relieve your stress or backache, then get some, place them on pressure points around your body, and focus on feeling good ... or do the same thing with Milk Duds. The item is irrelevant, because what you need is already in you. The stones and the Milk Duds are just serving as a helpful conduit to get your body and your mind working together.

Crystals are cool, they're nature's beauty, and they make much less of a mess than melting chocolate balls under your sheets, so if you like having them around, by all means, use them and enjoy them. Treat them as a welcome catalyst for harnessing your own power to heal.

Sage is something else you often see in spiritual shops, and it has a long and interesting history. The practice of burning sage goes back thousands of years to cultures all around the world. The ancient Romans and Greeks, Celtic druids, and indigenous peoples of the Amazon all used sage in ceremonies and for medicinal purposes. And locally, Native Americans have burned sage for centuries (called "smudging") as a way of cleansing a person, place, or thing of negative energy.

Does sage really get rid of negative energies? Yes and no, in my opinion. I think that negative energies only exist if we *allow* them (again, there's only the Law of Attraction, there's no Law of Assertion), so I don't think the sage is doing anything that we couldn't do ourselves with our minds (though, admittedly, I do like the idea of keeping a Binaca-size can of sage spray in my purse for occasional run-ins with assholes, creeps, and dipshits). Again, it falls in the placebo zone, which is perfectly fine.

If the sage is the conduit for our minds to believe that the negative energies are disappearing, then yes, the negative energies will disappear, and we can gladly credit the sage for helping.

I think we all appreciate acts and rituals that help us heal or rid ourselves of something unwanted. They feel satisfying and empowering. And whether it's the act laying someone to rest, graduating to something new, or running your ex's Phish shirt down the garbage disposal before tossing it in the trash, rituals usually make us feel good.

So while I appreciate that dear Ned helps my creativity flow, I think we'd all agree that my skills are coming from within me. As supportive as he is, it would be unfounded to give Ned more credit than he deserves for what I ultimately produce.

The same goes for these things we've discussed here.

While they may absolutely contribute to our healing and well-being ... ultimately, they're nothing without *you*.

chapter fourteen

***

the vibrational crockpot

I have the inspiration to write a cookbook.

My cookbook will showcase one of my favorite fascinations, Old-fashioned Midwestern cooking.

It will be packed with mouth-watering glossies of classic mayonaise, marshmallow, fish, pimento olive, and Jell-o recipes.

It will also include helpful tips on how to pair cheap fruit wines (Rhubarb ... is it a red? Is it a white? Is it even wine?) properly with various meatloaves and tater tot casseroles.

I want to fill it with recipies that make your Norwegian grandmother shout, "The Devil himself made this!" and "Christ on a cracker, that's good!"

I can see it now.

So how does the cookbook in my mind manifest into the hottest cookbook on shelves across America?

Well, that's where our vibrational crockpot comes in.

As we all go through life, we have experiences that cause us to throw desires or preferences into a swirling vibrational (not yet physically manifested) crockpot of what we want next in life. That crockpot is constantly changing and evolving. We have an experience which causes us to say, "Ok, I liked this, and I didn't like that. More of this next time, less of that," and our stew gets a refresh.

This process is what life is. We're always pursuing things that we think will make us happier. That's not discontentment, it's our evolution. It's what makes life worth living (if we ever get so uninspired or stagnant that we quit creating new dreams, might as well unplug the crockpot, stick our tongue in the socket, and drop dead).

Now most of the time, we are not a match to the dreams and desires we throw into our vibrational crockpot ... yet. They're just an inspired thought we have, like saying to yourself, "I want to write a cookbook."

That thought goes into the divine crockpot, and Source immediately answers back with a map, the tools, and the guidance for you to become a successful cookbook author (trust me, *infinite* intelligence knows people, who know people, who can help you with every detail).

Source really does work that way—you can have any dream become reality; there is nothing that Source can't pave the way for. Ask for it and ... Boom! ... you're on your way to becoming a successful cookbook author, discussing the culinary attributes of walleye calzones on morning talk shows across the country.

It's all there and waiting for you.

But the reason it feels like it's *not* there is because *you're* not there.

Because you're currently standing in your kitchen making deep-fried-pickle street tacos and thinking, *"It's a cool dream, but it will never happen for me."* It's not that the dream is too big, it's that your resistance is too strong.

Until you remove your resistance and begin *feeling* like a successful cookbook author, you can't match your own desire and attract it into your life.

Which brings up the obvious question, "But how am I supposed to *feel* like a successful cookbook author if I've *never been* a successful cookbook author?"

You get there by doing *whatever it takes* to get yourself into a positive emotional state of savoring what your crockpot dream will actually taste like.

Without going into specific details, go into your meditation closet and think about how warm and satisfying it will feel to see your cookbook in print. Purposely put words to the feelings that come up, "exciting, rewarding, meaningful, fun …"

Focus on finding positive, general thoughts about it while you're driving, when you're laying in bed, and when you have time to daydream. Create a vision board of photos and expressions that make you feel enlivened and optimistic about your dream, or even create some kind of unique gesture that raises your vibe—Jim Carrey wrote himself a ten million dollar check for "acting services rendered" and kept it in his wallet for years when he started his career (he's now worth $180 million).

Stay open and upbeat about it, *and for God's sake*, be choosy about who you share your divine crockpot dream with. Don't go sharing your desires with known dream-squelchers who will only add resistance to your perfect stew. And don't let your own ego creep in and throw a wet wool blanket over your plans if things don't flow perfectly or are slow to manifest.

Keep honing your craft and trust that clear inspiration to take your next step will appear when the time (vibe) is right. Respect and enjoy the evolutionary process of it all, and keep this in mind: The original Harry Potter was rejected twelve times before being published, and *Chicken Soup for the Soul* was rejected a whopping 144 times before it was published. It took Thomas Edison a thousand tries to get the light bulb right, Walt Disney was one million dollars in debt when he made *Snow White,* and a young Elvis Presley bombed on the stage of the *Grand Ole Opry* ... but I'd say things still turned out pretty well for all of those people because they maintained their expectations of success, even through the failures and slow times.

Everyone is worthy of living their biggest crockpot dreams, and Source can get you there ... *if* raise your own vibe enough for the Law of Attraction to match *you* to *your crockpot.*

The secret ingredient to manifesting your dreams is knowing you don't have to earn it or force it, rather, you just have to get yourself in a vibrational state that *attracts* it.

chapter fifteen

***

you had me at namaste

Chakras are supposed energy centers of the body. The exact origin of the concept isn't clear, but generally, the notion of chakras as we know it in the West today comes from a cross between Indian (specifically Hindu) tradition and the New Age movement (and again, I promised you I'd not get too serious in this book, so while chakras can be a broad, complex subject, I'm going to refer to them in generalities here).

Gretchen Stelter of Healthline.com explains chakras like this, "Chakra ... means "wheel" and refers to energy points in your body. They are thought to be spinning disks of energy that should stay "open" and aligned, as they correspond to bundles of nerves, major organs, and areas of our energetic body that affect our emotional and physical well-being. Some say there are

114 different chakras, but there are seven main chakras that run along your spine. These are the chakras that most of us are referring to when we talk about them."

Each of the seven main chakras has a corresponding number, name, color, specific area of the spine, and health focus. Chakras are what you're seeing on those posters of a sitting body figure with rainbow of dots going from the top of the head to the base of the spine.

From bottom to top the seven main chakras are:

The root chakra (#1, tailbone, red). A blocked root chakra can manifest as physical issues such as lower digestive problems, or emotionally through feelings of worry about having basic needs met.

The sacral chakra (#2, just below the belly button, orange). Issues here appear as problems with the nearby organs, including sexual organs. Emotionally, this chakra is connected to pleasure, sexuality, and creativity.

The solar plexus (#3, stomach area, yellow). Blockages in the third chakra are often experienced through upper digestive issues, like ulcers or indigestion. It's the chakra of self-confidence.

The heart chakra (#4, heart area, green). Unbalance here can manifest as heart problems and weight issues. When open, love flows freely; when blocked, one feels lonely and insecure.

The throat chakra (#5, throat area, light blue). This chakra is connected to our ability to articulate. A blocked throat chakra can manifest in weak communication and various health problems in this area.

The third eye chakra (#6, between the eyes, blue). Blockages here can surface as headaches and an emotionally closed mind.

When balanced, one sees the big picture.

The crown chakra (#7, top of the head, violet). When this chakra is open, it is thought to help keep all the other chakras open and flowing, which brings one bliss and enlightenment.

So, how do chakras get blocked or unbalanced?

Through life experience. An emotional upheaval of some type is usually the culprit—a job loss, a break up, a break down, financial uncertainty, etc.

Ok, I'm on board with chakras up to this point. Something unexpected happens, you're having emotional stress about it (which is normal—it's ok to *not* be ok at times), and now negative vibes are physically affecting your body in certain places. That makes sense; I've experienced that. And I can even say I've had moments in my life when, at the other end of the spectrum, I have felt unexplainable, pleasant tingling at the chakra points.

It's no big stretch for me to accept that chakras points in our body, while unseen, are real.

But beyond that is where my personal attention to the subject of chakras begins to wane. Because at this point, I usually read or hear that the solutions to unblock your chakras are things like having specific crystals around you, eating natural, chakra-color-corresponding foods (no, unfortunately Skittles, while perfectly suited for the job, apparently don't work), doing yoga, or having work done by a reiki practitioner (reiki comes from a Japanese tradition, where, through the hands, a healer transfers energy throughout a patient's body to encourage physical and emotional well-being).

And here again, without judgement, is where I'll bring up the word "placebo."

Since we can't just take our chakras to the dry cleaners, or have negative energy liposuction once a year, it's our responsibility to take care of them ourselves. And if blocked chakras originate with the mind, then logically, the only way to unblock them is *also* with the mind.

So, if crystals, yoga, and/or a session with a reiki practitioner helps persuade your mind that your chakra is balancing or unblocking ... than your mind will start relaying those positive vibes to your cells, your energy will begin to shift, and your problems *will* likely begin to disappear.

But, like I've said before, the results are still entirely dependent on *your* thoughts and beliefs on the subject.

Our natural state is emotional and physical well-being. We are all entitled and equipped, per the ginormous mass of love energy, to live with healthy minds and bodies.

All that ever gets in the way of our own well-being is ourselves, which goes back to resistance. Blockages are just symptoms of resistance. Clear the resistance and well-being is always there (i.e. the sun is always shining, the clouds just need to part for it to be seen).

And again, how can we clear resistance? By grieving, venting, and sleeping, when that's the best we can do. By meditating, getting into nature, aimlessly losing ourselves down YouTube rabbit holes for an hour ... and by using placebos. All of which are doing the same thing, refocusing our attention off our problems (the clouds) for long enough to welcome well-being (the sun) back again.

Chakras are just another aspect of spirituality that you hear about often. Go with your gut (aka, sacral chakra) and your own experience on this one.

And while we're on the subject, let's talk about two other Eastern norms that we've Westernized, the word *namaste,* and the concept of karma.

The use of *namaste* has grown by leaps and bounds in the West. Western yoga teachers have been increasingly using it at the end of classes, with good intentions, to convey, "The divine light in me bows to the divine light in you."

But, to most modern Hindi (from which it originated) speakers, it's not a blessing or something you say when parting, it's just a slightly formal greeting for "Hello."

While it's original meaning was "I bend to you," it's now simply used to properly greet someone whom you don't know very well or who is older than you (it's akin to saying a more formal "Hello," versus a casual "Hi," to someone in English).

In Hindi, *namaste* is not some mystical word that gets you the keys to the executive washroom of spirituality or makes you sound holy.

It's just "Hello."

That's all.

And since putting "*Hello,* bitches!" on bumper stickers, tee-shirts, and water bottles would be so unclever that it's confusing to even us, then maybe we should probably, in the name of good humor and cultural sensitivity, stop doing the same with *namaste.*

While the jury is out on whether it's wrong to use a foreign word incorrectly, so long as you're not using it offensively, I suspect Hindi speakers could argue that it's offensive that it's being used incorrectly, *period.*

So, you make the call.

If you want, in a spontaneous romantic moment, to tell your new 7-11 lover, *"You had me at namaste,"* I support that.

Use it, just try to use it correctly, I say.

Our third Eastern belief that's been Western-tweaked over time is the concept of karma.

In the Eastern traditions, karma (also called dharma in some context), like chakras, can get very complex and detailed. Eastern karma beliefs essentially say that your actions in one life (good or bad) affect your circumstance in the next life. While I do believe in reincarnation, I don't believe in the idea of karma carrying over from lifetime to lifetime. My spiritual understanding tells me that the present is all that really matters—everything's happening in the now—so the idea that I'd ever be vibrationally attracting something right now as a consequence for something that I did in a past life, *that I don't even remember,* doesn't compute for me.

So, while I respect that karma carrying over through lifetimes is the belief of billions of people, it's just not one that I share.

I think it's fair to say that in the West, the word "karma" has morphed into borderline slang, used to loosely label evidence of "what goes around comes around."

And I think most Westerners (without having beliefs in reincarnation) treat karma as only relevant to the life they're *currently* in.

I do align with the core principle of karma, in that we reap what we sow. And frankly, that's not religious or spiritual, that's just the Law of Attraction at work. You get what back what you put out.

I don't believe karma is something that is passed down to you via judgement from a higher source, rather it's just the natural consequence of how our thoughts and actions are reflected back to us in life. Karma, in that sense, is a useful tool for measuring where you're vibrationally at on certain subjects—just look at what you're attracting, and you'll see what your thought and beliefs are projecting.

I will admit, sometimes our karma (aka, what we've attracted per the Law of Attraction) doesn't seem to make sense … at the time. Sometimes you give a project, a job, or a relationship your all, only to see it unexpectedly go down in flames. And while the temptation at the time may be to wail out your bedroom window through a bullhorn, "Whaaaaat did I dooooo to deserve thissssssss?" I suggest hanging on a little longer and seeing what comes next. What you see as misfortune now, very often is a just new path appearing. A path to something even better than what you've been living.

Stay positive. What looks like bad karma may actually be good karma in the big picture.

So, in a nutshell, on these subjects … make up your own mind on chakras … and think it through before you next *namaste* someone.

It's just good karma.

chapter sixteen

***

the times they are a changin'

Well my friends, I think we've come to the end of our journey for now. Please gather up all your personal belongings and souveniers and prepare to exit to your left.

Strangely enough, with a little help from Petey "The Chicken Killer" dachshund, the Dalai Lama, and James Bond, I believe we just successfully covered awakening, death, meditation, religion, psychics, tarot, astrology, resistance, yoga, jerks, crystals, vibrations, meat, chakras, namaste, karma, and a few other spiritual odds and ends (and as I mentioned when we started, if you want to learn more about the Law of Attraction, soulmates, synchronicities, numerology, and the ego, then check out *Hippie Dippy Bulls**t*).

I hope our adventure inspired you to question what you

believe and to go explore more.

For myself, what I discovered as I dug deeper into these subjects is that it all comes down to one thing: Me.

While some things we discussed here may be useful catalysts, rituals, or placebos, they're no substitute for the power of the ginormous mass of love energy that's within me, and you, to heal from, accomplish, or have anything we desire. Our connection to Source, and our thoughts and beliefs, will *always* be the most important factor in determining our well-being and the outcome of our experiences.

Which is good news. It's means we're in control much more than we think. Take that knowledge to heart, and eagerly choose your thoughts and emotions deliberately, with purpose and with optimism.

I believe there's a mass, evolutionary shift happening of folks like us. I think we're only going to see more and more people moving out of the dogmatic religions of their ancestors, into a personal practice of spirituality. Thankfully, we're no longer reliant on just a handful of written teachings from the past to learn and choose from. We have available to us, right now, an abundance of first-hand, perfectly recorded teachings from master teachers, still living, who've experienced enlightenment at the top of the ladder.

And I, personally, think great things are going to come from that.

Yes, friends, the times they are a changin' … and I'm glad to be part of that with you.

So until next time, this is your not-too-serious, donut-eating, mattress-naming tour guide, thanking you for coming along on this spiritual adventure and reminding you that the continuing journey is yours to, powerfully and playfully, go forth and create.

Made in the USA
Monee, IL
26 May 2022